FEDERAL RESERVE

THE UNITED STATES OF AMERICA

THIS BOOK BELONGS TO:

_____

This book was gifted to _____ from _____.

Then _____ gifted this book to _____.

Value Knowledge. Gift it Forward.........

IN GOD WE TRUST

ONE DOLLAR

Preface

The experience of raising children has created a real desire in both my wife, Febyolla and me to help our kids understand the foundation of money and its roots. To our family money is a valued tool! It is not the purpose of mankind to live for the Almighty buck. The buck lets us own our own time, provides shelter, food and other necessities. To some, it is the existence of life. To us, in our house, we do not live to work. As hard as we work, we still play harder and enjoy the simple times of life with family and friends.

This book is for you and your children to enjoy together, while you teach your kids to understand the basics of the buck. We then invite you to Gift the Knowledge Forward.

WRITTEN BY Dustin Goss

ILLUSTRATED BY Febyolla Goss

DEDICATED TO

Our son **Dusty**, our daughter **Marvel**

and the minds of tomorrow...

Reading & Interaction Tips:

Prepare one of each coin...

Penny

Nickel

Dime

Quarter

...and a clean dollar bill to interact with while you read.

*Prewash the coins & bill so they are clean for use over and over again.

Money Saver

Table of Contents

Chapter I

This is a story about money

and making sense of the buck.....

Money has value and is a creation that we use to trade for goods and services. Most countries in the world use bills and coins as money. Each country has its own name for its money. In the USA we call our money the Dollar. Let's learn more about our money with BUCK.

Meet our friend Buck......

Buck is a Dollar Bill.

The buck is a common nickname for a dollar!

Let's learn more about Buck and his friends!

What cents do they have......

What are they worth......

What do they look like......

IN GOD WE TRUST

ONE DOLLAR

The most valued friends closest to Buck are called...

¢oins!

Let's meet Buck's coin friends......

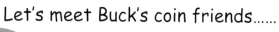

Buck has four regular coins that hang out with him.

Penny   Nickel   Dime   Quarter

Each coin is......

> worth a different value
>
> > looks different
> >
> > > and comes in a different size.

These characteristics of each coin make them unique just like you and me.

IN GOD WE TRUST

ONE DOLLAR

Each COIN has two sides...

 The first side is called **"Heads"**

 The second side is called **"Tails"**

Coins are valued in cents and use the symbol.

Bills or Bucks are valued in dollars and use the symbol.

Meet Penny.....

The Penny is worth **1¢** or **$0.01**

The Penny is copper-colored and has smooth edges. The "heads" side has an image of Abraham Lincoln. And most Pennies have an image of the Lincoln Memorial on the "tails" side, unless it was minted after 2010; then it has the Union Shield on it.

Heads Up

Abraham Lincoln was the 16th US President who was most famous for preserving the Union during the Civil War and for abolishing slavery. What year is your penny?

Tails Up

The Lincoln Memorial is located in Washington DC. The Shield represents Lincoln's preservation of the United States as a single country.

Meet Nickel.....

The Nickel is worth **5¢** or **$0.05**

The Nickel is silver in color and has smooth edges all the way around. The "heads" side has an image of Thomas Jefferson and the "tails" side has an image of the building known as Monticello.

Heads Up

Thomas Jefferson was the 3rd U.S. president and is most famous for his contribution in writing the Declaration of Independence.

Tails Up

Monticello was Thomas Jefferson's house that he designed himself. It is located in the state of Virginia.

Meet Dime.....

The Dime is worth 10¢ or $0.10

The Dime is silver-colored and has 118 ridges around its edge. The "heads" side has an image of Franklin D. Roosevelt and the "tails" side has images of an olive branch, a torch, and an oak tree branch.

Heads Up

Franklin D Roosevelt or FDR was the 32nd U.S. president and the only president to serve four terms in office. He led the United States through World War II and the 'Great Depression.'

Tails Up

What do the images on the Dime stand for?

> **Olive Branch** - stands for Peace
>
> **Torch** - stands for Liberty
>
> **Oak Branch** - stands for Strength & Independence

Meet Quarter.....

The Quarter is worth **25¢** or **$0.25**

The Quarter is silver-color and has 119 ridges around its edge. The "heads" side has an image of George Washington. The "tails" side has an image of an Eagle; after 1999, the Liberty Quarter was introduced, with the "tails" side has 50 different images representing our 50 states.

Heads Up

George Washington was the 1st U.S. president. He was the General who led the American Revolution and created the team who wrote the US Constitution.

Tails Up

Before 1999, the Quarter has the 'presidential coat of arms,' which is the Eagle with stretched wings. The 1999 and beyond Quarter has 50 unique versions that tell a piece of a state's story.

So what about Buck?

You met Buck's friends, the coins, and learned about...
their heads, tails, and values.

The Buck is worth **100¢** or **$1.00** or **1** Buck.

A Buck or Dollar is a "paper" bill that is used as money. It is untraditional paper as it is really 75% Cotton & 25% Linen. The Buck has an image of George Washington on the front and an image of a pyramid and an eagle on the back.

Front

George Washington was an American hero and our 1st U.S. president from 1789 to 1797. He is sometimes referred to as the "Father of our Country."

Back

Look at the Eagle's talons closely. It is holding an olive branch in the right (representing peace) and arrows in its left (symbolizing war). Do you see the "Eye of Providence"? It is surrounded by rays of light and enclosed by a triangle. It represents the eye of God watching over humanity.

Do You Know quiz: *What coin is George Washington on?*

Chapter II

How many ¢ents can a Buck buy?

IN GOD WE TRUST

ONE DOLLAR

Twenty-Five Cents

25¢ is a Quarter

Four Quarters equal one dollar.

How many Quarters can a Buck buy?

IN GOD WE TRUST

ONE DOLLAR

Ten Cents

10¢ is a Dime

Ten Dimes equal one dollar.

How many Dimes can a Buck buy?

 =

IN GOD WE TRUST

ONE DOLLAR

Answer: 10

Five Cents

5¢ is a Nickel

Twenty Nickels equal one dollar.

How many Nickels can a Buck buy?

=

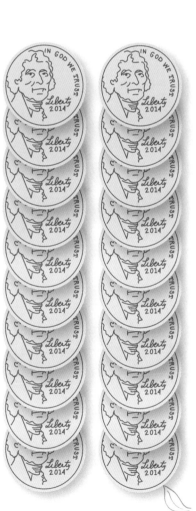

Answer: 20

IN GOD WE TRUST

ONE DOLLAR

One Cent

1¢ is a Penny

One Hundred cents equal one dollar.

How many Pennies can a Buck buy?

=

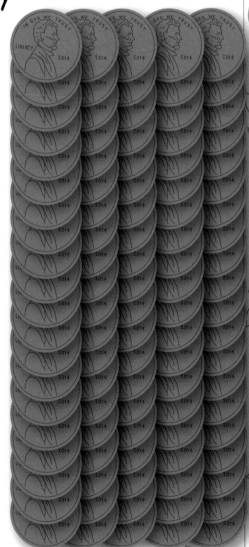

Answer: 100

IN GOD WE TRUST

ONE DOLLAR

Chapter III

Now you know what kind of cents a buck has.....

.....and how many cents can buy a buck!

Let's check your memory bank.....

Penny Check

If I save a penny a day, how many days till I have a Buck?

Per Day =

CALENDAR

Monday	Tuesday	Wednesday	Thursday	Friday	Saturday	Sunday
1	2	3	4	5	6	7
8	9	10	11	12	13	14
15	16	17	18	19	20	21
22	23	24	25	26	27	28
29	30	31				

How many days until I have a dollar?

Answer: 100

Nickel Check

Which coin is LARGER...

A Nickel or a Dime?

In Value...?

In Size...?

Answers:

The Dime is larger in value.
The Nickel is larger in size.

Dime Check

How many  equal a ?

How many equal a ?

Answers:

How many Nickels equal a Dime? 2

How many Pennies equal a Dime? 10

Page **24**

Quarter Check

What president is on the head side of a Quarter?

How many  equal 25¢ ?

Answers:
George Washington
How many Nickels equal a Quarter? 5

Page **25**

IN GOD WE TRUST

BUCK Check

How many dollars is a Buck worth?

How many of each coin does it take to equal a dollar?

=

Answers: A dollar is worth one buck.

100 pennies equal a Buck.

20 Nickels equal a Buck.

10 Dimes equal a Buck.

4 Quarters equal a Buck.

IN GOD WE TRUST

ONE DOLLAR

US Coin Fun Facts

The **Penny** has the only president facing to the right. Did you know the average life of a penny is 40 years!

The **Nickel** is the thickest coin in regular circulation. The new Nickel head's side now has Thomas Jefferson facing forward.

The **Dime** is the second most valuable regular issue coin, yet it is the smallest, thinnest, and lightest. Before 1965, it was made from real silver - so keep your eyes out for old dimes.

The **Quarter** was made out of real silver before 1965. Its ridges were designed to stop people from scraping the silver down to melt and sell.

US Dollar Bill Fun Facts

The average life of a **$1** bill or Buck is **5.8 years**.

As of 2017, there was **$12.1 Billion** Dollars worth of one dollar bills in circulation...Thats a lot of Bucks!

A **$1** bill or Buck cost **4.9 cents** cents to print.

The 'one' dollar bill has lots of nicknames...

1. Buck
2. One
3. Single
4. Greenback
5. Bone
6. Bill
7. Clam

Where has your dollar been? You can track your dollar bill online at www.wheresgeorge.com try it out.....

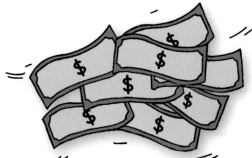